# nangarhar

**PROVINCIAL HANDBOOK** / A Guide to the People and the Province

## Nangarhar

- Paved Road
- District Border
- River
- Provincial Center
- City

LOWER ELEVATION — HIGHER ELEVATION

Kunar

Pakistan

Laghman

Kabul

Logar

Paktya

Lalpora

Dur Baba

Goshta

Basawol

Marko

Shinwar

Morchal

Nader Shah Kot

Jaba

Sra Kala

Sangarsari

Kala Shahi

Khewa

Jalalabad

Hesarshahi

Haskamena

Sultanpur

Chaparhar

Agam

Koga

Mamakhil

Regeh

# Table of Contents

# List of Tables and Maps

**LIST OF TABLES**

**LIST OF MAPS**

# Acronyms and Key Terms

| | |
|---|---|
| ABP | Afghan Border Police |
| ACNP | Afghan Counter Narcotics Police |
| ADP/E | Alternative Development Program for the Eastern Zone |
| ADT | Agribusiness Development Team |
| AICC | Afghanistan International Chamber of Commerce |
| AISA | Afghanistan Investment Services Association |
| ANA | Afghan National Army |
| ANP | Afghan National Police |
| AWCC | Afghan Wireless Communication Company |
| BEFA | Basic Education for Afghanistan |
| BHC | Basic Health Center |
| CA | Civil Affairs |
| CDC | Community Development Council |
| CERP | Commander's Emergency Response Program |
| CHC | Comprehensive Health Center |
| CID | Criminal Investigation Division |
| COIN | Counterinsurgency |
| CSO | Central Statistics Office |
| DDS | District Development Shura |
| DIAG | Disbandment of Illegal Armed Groups |
| DoS | US Department of State |
| FATA | Federally Administered Tribal Areas |
| FOB | Forward Operating Base |
| GIRoA | Government of the Islamic Republic of Afghanistan |
| HIG or HIH | Hezb-e Islami Gulbuddin ("Islamic Party" formed by Gulbuddin Hekmatyar) |
| HIK | Hezb-e Islami Khalis ("Islamic Party" formed by Mohammad Yunus Khalis) |
| HP | Health Posts |
| HTS | Human Terrain System |

| | |
|---|---|
| ICRC | International Committee of the Red Cross |
| IDLG | Independent Directorate for Local Governance |
| IED | Improvised Explosive Device |
| IMC | International Medical Corps |
| IO | International Organization |
| IRoA | Islamic Republic of Afghanistan |
| ISAF | International Security Assistance Force |
| ISI | Inter-Services Intelligence (Pakistan) |
| Jamiatis or JI | Jamiat-e Islami ("Islamic Union") |
| MADERA | Mission d'Aide des Economies Rural Afghanistan |
| Meshrano Jirga | Elders' Assembly, upper house of Afghan National Assembly |
| MRRD | Ministry of Rural Rehabilitation and Development |
| MoE | Ministry of Education |
| MoI | Ministry of the Interior |
| MoPH | Ministry of Public Health |
| MoPW | Ministry of Public Works |
| Mustafiat | Department of Finance |
| NATO | North Atlantic Treaty Organization |
| NDS | National Directorate for Security |
| NGO | Non-Governmental Organization |
| NSP | National Solidarity Program |
| NWFP | North West Frontier Province |
| PC | Provincial Council |
| PDC | Provincial Development Council |
| PRT | Provincial Reconstruction Team |
| RAH | Reconstruction Agency of Hindu Kush |
| SCA | Swedish Committee for Afghanistan |
| UN | United Nations |
| UNAMA | United Nations Assistance Mission in Afghanistan |
| UNOPS | United Nations Office for Project Services |
| USACE | US Army Corp of Engineers |
| USAID | US Agency for International Development |
| USDA | US Department of Agriculture |
| USG | United States Government |
| VOA | Voice of America |
| Wali | Governor |
| Wolesi Jirga | People's Assembly, lower house of Afghan National Assembly |
| Woluswal | District Administrator |

# Guide to the Handbook

This handbook is a concise field guide to Nangarhar for internationals deploying to the province. Field personnel have used these guides in Afghanistan since June 2008 to accelerate their orientation process and to serve as a refresher on different aspects of the province during their tour.

Reading this book will provide a basic understanding of the people, places, history, culture, politics, economy, needs, and ideas of Kunar. Building upon this understanding can help you:

- build rapport and a regular dialogue with local leaders,
- plan and implement pragmatic strategies (security, political, economic) to address sources of instability,
- influence communities to support the political process, not the insurgents, and
- build the capacity and legitimacy of a self-sufficient Afghan government and economy.

As you read the handbook and continue your inquiry in the province, seek to understand the influential leaders and groups in your local area and what beliefs and relationships drive their behavior. Think about the sources of violence in the area and whether groups are pursuing interests in a way that promotes conflict or stability. Finally, consider how various types of activities – key leader engagement, development assistance, security operations, security assistance, or public diplomacy – can effectively influence communities to work within the political process and oppose insurgency.

## SOURCES AND METHODS

These handbooks are not intended as original academic research but as concise, readable summaries for practitioners in the field. The editorial team relies on their collective field experience and knowledge of the province as well as key sources such as the official Islamic Republic of Afghanistan (IRoA), United Nations, and United States Government (USG) publications and those sources listed in the appendix.

The editors made every effort to ensure accuracy. It should be noted, however, that there is often considerable disagreement regarding what is "ground truth" in Nangarhar, and things are constantly changing. As such, consider this book part of your orientation, and not an all-inclusive source for everything you need to know.

Information in this handbook is unclassified. The views and opinions expressed in this handbook are those of IDS International and in no way reflect the views of the United States Government or the United States Army.

## THE ELECTRONIC UPDATE

Look for electronic updates to this book at *www.idsinternational.net/ afpakbooks*. Updates will cover any new developments, issues, and leaders that have emerged after publication. They will also provide corrections and expanded content in key areas based on feedback from readers.

We hope the handbook will continue to be a valuable tool in thinking about the challenges in Nangarhar. If you have questions, comments, or feedback for future updates or editions please email *afpakbooks@idsinternational.net*.

## ABOUT IDS INTERNATIONAL

**Publisher of Afghanistan Provincial Handbook Series and the FATA/NWFP Pakistan Books**

This book is one of a series of handbooks on Afghanistan provinces and regions of Pakistan. Titles include Ghazni, Helmand, Kandahar, Khost, Kunar, Laghman, Nangarhar, Nuristan, Paktya, and Paktika. Pakistan titles include NWFP and FATA.

In addition to publishing these handbooks, IDS International provides training and analysis to government and private organizations in the areas of politics, economics, culture, stability operations, reconstruction, counterinsurgency, and interagency relations. In particular, IDS is a leading trainer of the US military in working with Provincial Reconstruction Teams (PRTs) in Iraq and Afghanistan. IDS offers its clients expertise and experience in the difficult work of interagency collaboration in complex operations. The writers and editors on this project offer a lifetime of experience working in these provinces and share a dedication to bringing peace and prosperity to the people of Afghanistan.

**Author:** Chris Corsten
**Editors:** Nick Dowling and Tom Praster
**Assistant Editors:** Tom Viehe and Katie Stout

**IDS INTERNATIONAL GOVERNMENT SERVICES**

1916 Wilson Boulevard

Suite 302

Arlington, VA 22201

703-875-2212

*www.idsinternational.net*

*afpakbooks@idsinternational.net*

**PUBLISHED: JUNE 2009**

This and other AfPak handbooks may be bought in either hard copy, digital, or audiobook format. Samples are available upon request. IDS International is also a leading provider of training and support on the cultural, political, economic, interagency, and information aspects of conflict. Direct all inquires to *afpakbooks@idsinternational.net* or call 703-875-2212

*Host to some of the largest and most diverse markets in eastern Afghanistan, the streets of Jalalabad are congested with large trucks, tiny three-wheeled ricksha taxis, donkey-drawn carts, and the ubiquitous beat-up Toyota Corolla. It is easy to pick up Pakistani gold, Japanese televisions, and Nangarhari oranges all in one trip.*

PHOTO BY NICK DOWLING

# Chapter 1
# Overview and Orientation

Nangarhar province is a land of beautiful contrasts. The rugged snowcapped mountains and barren hills give way to streaks of green, lush valleys and rivers that both trickle and flood with the passing of the seasons. The agricultural land is lined with a dizzying maze of intricate irrigation canals fed from the mountain streams. Thousands of *jeribs* of arable land bring a bounty of wheat, vegetables, and fruits from the newly planted orchards. The larger swaths of farmland are irrigated from a major dam-and-canal structure that runs west to east from Jalalabad to Ghanikhel. The mountains to the west and south of the province contain vast marble and gem deposits that are now starting to show commercial potential. Most major road systems are either paved or under construction, making travel much safer and quicker than only a couple of years ago. However, many outlying areas still rely on dangerous dirt trails that would rival any off-road competition course. These roads have kept government and outside influences from extending their reach into the most reclusive areas.

The streets in Jalalabad are clogged with traffic during the day, with everything from large trucks to tiny three-wheeled ricksha taxis and donkey-drawn carts. The larger highways are filled with enormous, elaborately painted trucks (called "jingle trucks" due to the sound the decorative metal fringe creates) carrying oversized loads between Pakistan and Kabul. Outlying villages use 4x4 trucks and beat-up Toyota Corollas to navigate the unimproved roads. In these small villages, tribal hospitality is the norm. You will usually be welcomed and treated as a guest of honor with green tea, flat bread, lamb, and fresh vegetables and surrounded by older men who are happy to talk about local gossip, their past fights with the Soviets, and their new problems.

Nearly all goods entering or exiting the country's eastern border will pass through Nangarhar. Jalalabad, its capital, hosts some of the largest and most diverse markets in eastern Afghanistan, where it is easy to pick up Pakistani gold, Japanese televisions, and Nangarhari oranges in a single shopping trip. Agriculture is the primary occupation in Nangarhar, but marble production and carpet weaving are also common. Illegally generated income is largely tied to smuggling and the opium industry. In the past two years, Nangarhar's opium poppy cultivation has dropped to negligible levels.

Nangarharis have a history of supporting insurgents. During the first Anglo-Afghan war, the British had their last stand at Gandamak in western Nangarhar. Only one man survived this infamous retreat in which nearly 16,000 soldiers and followers were killed, foreshadowing what mujahedin fighters would do against the Soviets a century later. The turning point of the anti-Soviet war occurred at the Jalalabad airport, when Stinger missiles were first used to destroy Soviet helicopters. Osama bin Laden was welcomed at the Jalalabad airport in 1996, and he joined forces with the Taliban a few months later. Still, in 2001, many Nangarharis supported US forces and the Northern Alliance against the Taliban. This support largely continues today, although insurgents find refuge in some areas.

## ORIENTATION

Nangarhar is located in the Eastern Region of Afghanistan and shares borders with Kunar province in the northeast, Laghman province in the north, Kabul in the west, Logar in the southwest, and the Federally

Administered Tribal Areas (FATA) of Pakistan in the east and south. Nangarhar has mountainous areas along all of its borders. The populated areas are mainly situated along rivers and streams. The Kabul and Kunar Rivers water the province. The main thoroughfare between Kabul and Pakistan follows an east-west trajectory along the Kabul River through Nangarhar and the ancient Khyber Pass. The province covers 7,616 square kilometers. Eighty-seven percent of the population lives in rural areas.

## Districts

The province consists of 22 recognized districts and one unofficial district, Spinghar. Spinghar district is recognized by the local Shinwari tribe and the Nangarhar government but is not recognized by the central government and international community. Each district has a district center, with a compound including facilities for district governor, his staff, and other key district offices.

## Key Towns

**Jalalabad** is Nangarhar's provincial capital. The largest city in eastern Afghanistan and a cultural jewel, it has long been considered the region's economic, social, and political hub. It has beautiful gardens, tree-lined avenues, and an annual poetry festival in honor of the orange blossoms. The peace of the past few years has allowed the city to transform from a run-down town of mud structures and poor infrastructure to a more modern city. Large office buildings are being built throughout the downtown, and the main roads through the city are now paved. The Provincial Reconstruction Team (PRT) has begun an extensive side street paving plan with drainage to stop sewage backups. If the current pace continues, Jalalabad will be an exemplar of economic development in the next five years.

There are five towns of note outside of Jalalabad City:

**Kaga, Khogiani District:** This town is the district center and main trading hub for the Khogiani tribe. The town has a large bazaar area with several shops and paved roads through the main thoroughfare. The road to Jalalabad is now paved, which makes transportation of goods and services more effective. This town also has the only hospital in western Nangarhar. To improve stability, there is a US military base near the town.

**Ghanikhel, Shinwar District:** The "capital" of the Shinwari tribe, Ghanikhel sits at the mouth of the primary trade route with the province's south-eastern districts. It also has a paved road linking it to Jalalabad via Highway 1. Ghanikhel is often the site of protests against the government and US forces when operations are conducted in the Shinwari areas. During these protests, locals tend to block the main road with stones and sometimes block Highway 1 to the north. The town is the headquarters of the border police battalion in eastern Nangarhar. The town also hosts a hospital and a large bazaar.

**Torkham, Momandara District:** Torkham is located at the Afghan-Pakistan border crossing. This hub of commerce and trade is the first stop into Afghanistan from the Torkham Gate, the second-largest border crossing in the country.

Note: Kaga, Ghanikhel, and Torkham are municipalities, with individual mayors who all answer to the Jalalabad mayor's office.

**Marko, Shinwar District:** This town is often called Marko Bazaar and is the main trading hub in eastern Nangarhar. The bazaar consists of several small shops strung along Highway 1, five kilometers north of Ghanikhel. The highway is being widened into a four-lane, divided highway from the Pakistani border all the way to Jalalabad, although progress has stopped due to lack of funds. Due to this, Marko Bazaar is being ripped up and rebuilt on the north side of the highway. The area is often congested due to heavy truck traffic and cars stopping on the road to buy goods.

**Khewa, Koz Kunar District:** The town of Khewa is the district center of Koz Kunar district and is the main trading hub north of Jalalabad. It also serves as the main meeting place for the Pashai in Nangarhar. The town has a large bazaar with a paved road linking it to Jalalabad and Asadabad, the capital of Kunar province to the north. This town is in a relatively peaceful area of Nangarhar and benefits from the many NGOs working on its road and irrigation systems. The town is easily in range of the produce markets in Jalalabad, making it a relatively prosperous area.

## RELEVANT HISTORICAL ISSUES

### From Ancient to Modern Times

In 1570, the Mogul Emperor Jalaluddin Akbar founded a city he called Jalalabad, or "Abode of Splendor." Since then, every invading army that has crossed the Khyber Pass from the east went to Kabul via Jalalabad. With its pleasant climate, most of the rich and powerful maintained winter homes in Nangarhar. Amir Habibullah, the reform-minded king of Afghanistan from 1901-1919, had the Palace Seraj-ul-Emorat constructed in 1910. He and his successor, King Amanullah, are buried in the large mausoleum in the city center.

The most important issue in regional dynamics is the Durand Line, the disputed border drawn in 1893 by British official Sir Mortimer Durand, which divided the Pashtun heartland. The Afghan king who signed the treaty claimed he did so under duress, making the border invalid. In 1994, many Pashtuns claimed the 100-year old treaty expired. Many tribes straddling the border only acknowledge it when it serves their purposes.

## Table 1. District Populations

| DISTRICT | CENTER | POPULATION | TRIBES |
|---|---|---|---|
| Achin | Sra Kala | 150,000 | Shinwari |
| Bati Kot | Nader Shah Kot | 285,000 | Mohmand, Shinwari |
| Behsood | Khusgumband | 180,000 | Mixed |
| Chaparhar | Chaparhar | 53,400 | Mixed |
| Dari Nur | Kala Shahi | 100,000 | Pashai |
| Deh Bala | Haskamena | 150,000 | Shinwari |
| Dur Baba | Dur Baba | 57,000 | Shinwari |
| Goshta | Goshta | 64,200 | Mohmand |
| Hesarak | Regeh | 27,200 | Ahmadzai |
| Jalalabad | Jalalabad | 200,367 | Mixed |
| Kama | Sangarsari | 170,000 | Mohmand |
| Khogiani | Kaga | 229,000 | Khogiani |
| Kot | Jaba | 135,000 | Mohmand |
| Koz Kunar | Khewa | 120,000 | Pashai |
| Lalpur | Lalpura | 50,000 | Mohmand |
| Momandara | Basawol | 128,000 | Mohmand |
| Nazyan | Morchal | 70,000 | Shinwari |
| Pachir Wa Agam | Agam | 75,000 | Khogiani |
| Rodat | Hesarshahi | 120,000 | Mohmand |
| Sherzad | Mamakhil | 58,800 | Khogiani |
| Shinwar | Ghanikhel | 164,000 | Shinwari |
| Spinghar | Sra Kala | w/ Achin | Shinwari |
| Surkh Rod | Sultanpur | 150,000 | Ahmadzai |
| **Total** | | **2,736,967** | |

## Communist Era (1979-1992)

Military action in Nangarhar in the Soviet period consisted mostly of small attacks at night by the mujahedin, followed by massive retaliation by the Soviets. The turning point of the war occurred in Jalalabad, where the mujahedin destroyed three Soviet helicopters with US-supplied Stinger missiles in 1986. For the first time, Afghans were able to take out their greatest threat.

During this period, two key mujahedin factions became influential: Hezb-e Islami (Gulbadin Hekmatyar (HIG)) and a splinter group of HIG called Hezb-e Islami Khales (HIK). Partnering with Pakistan's Directorate of Inter-Services Intelligence (ISI) during the Soviet-Afghan war, HIG became a powerful political-military entity. Led by Yunis Khales, HIK split off from HIG a few years later and gained support of many key tribal families in Nangarhar.

## Mujahedin and Taliban (1992-2001)

After the 1992 collapse of the communist government, Nangarhar was under the control of the Jalalabad Shura, headed by HIK's Haji Abdul Qadir. In Spring 1996, Osama Bin Laden was permitted to settle in Nangarhar. In August 1996, Taliban supporters, aided by Pakistani intelligence, swarmed westward out of Pakistan to join a Taliban column coming from the south. Qadir fled to Pakistan with most of the other mujahedin commanders. By September, Nangarhar, Kunar, and Laghman provinces were in Taliban hands. Within days, the Taliban forced the Northern Alliance to abandon Kabul, and bin Laden shifted his allegiance to the Taliban.

The Taliban was supported in the east mainly because it brought stability, but was otherwise far too radical for most Nangarharis. The Taliban were mostly out of Nangarhar by November 2001. Fighting moved to the Tora Bora section of the Spin Ghar (White Mountains) in southern Nangarhar. Three leaders fought for control: Hazrat Ali; Haji Qadir, the pre-Taliban governor of Nangarhar; and Haji Zaman, a mujahedin commander from Khogiani. The interim government appointed Haji Qadir to the governorship and Hazrat Ali as provincial police chief. Haji Zaman was run out of Nangarhar, due in large part to Hazrat Ali's lobbying efforts. Haji Qadir was

# Map 1. Population Map of Nangarhar

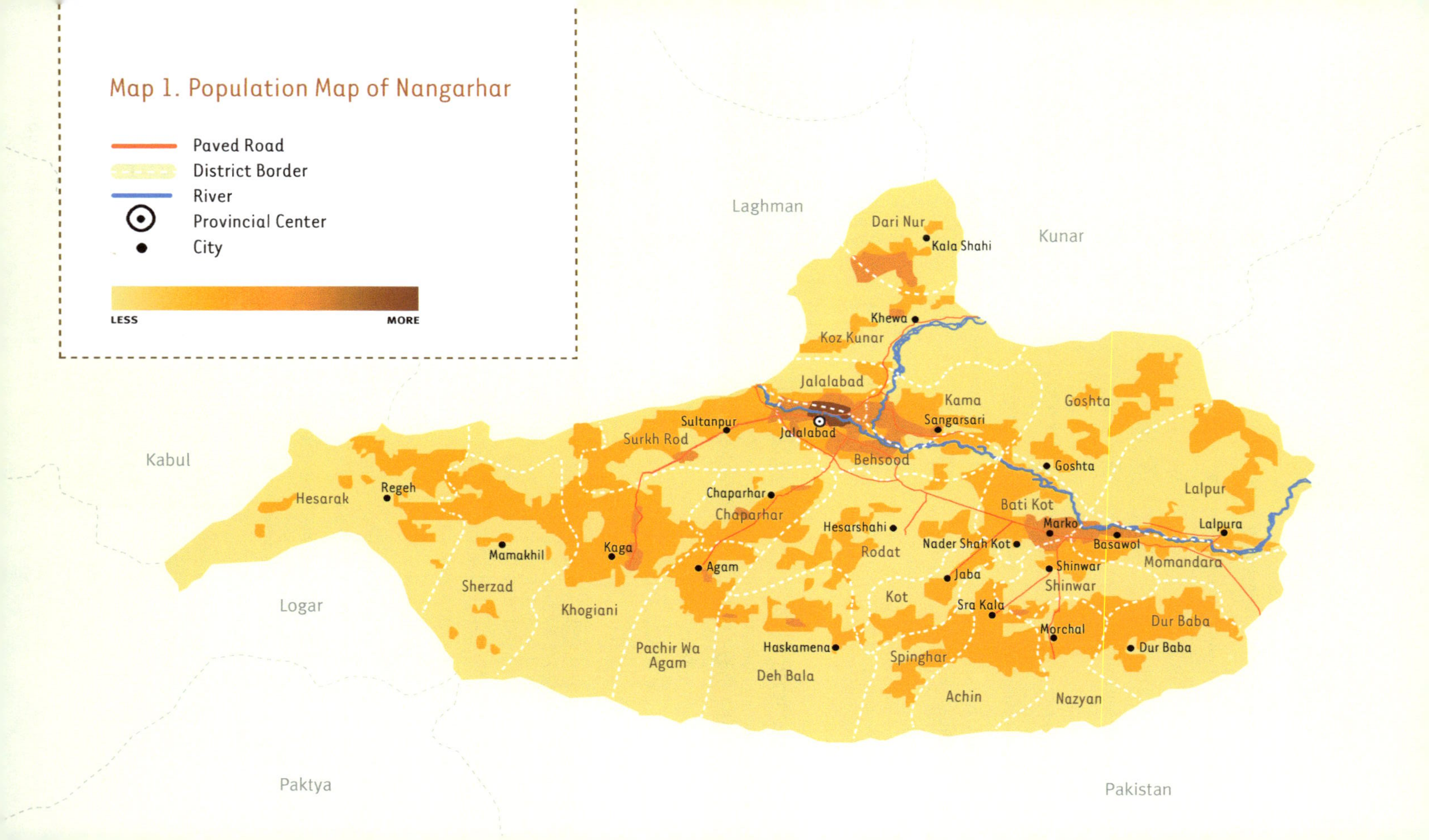

**Legend**

- Paved Road
- District Border
- River
- ⊙ Provincial Center
- ● City

LESS — MORE

Pakistan

Kunar

Laghman

Kabul

Logar

Paktya

Lalpur
Lalpura
Momandara
Dur Baba
Dur Baba
Goshta
Goshta
Basawol
Marko
Bati Kot
Shinwar
Shinwar
Morchal
Nazyan
Kala Shahi
Dari Nur
Kama
Sangarsari
Nader Shah Kot
Jaba
Sra Kala
Achin
Khewa
Koz Kunar
Behsood
Hesarshahi
Rodat
Kot
Spinghar
Jalalabad
Jalalabad
Chaparhar
Chaparhar
Agam
Haskamena
Deh Bala
Sultanpur
Surkh Rod
Kaga
Pachir Wa Agam
Khogiani
Mamakhil
Sherzad
Regeh
Hesarak

promoted to governor of Nangarhar, but he was murdered in Kabul in 2002. His brother, Haji Din Mohammed, then took over Nangarhar's governorship.

## Contemporary Events (2002-present)

In the 2004 elections, Nangarhar voted largely for Hamid Karzai. Karzai's plan to end poppy cultivation had a significant impact on Nangarhar, and poppy growth dropped by 96 percent in 2005. Since 2005, poppy growing has ebbed and flowed in response to the population's frustration with economic alternatives and the continued illegal poppy cultivation in other provinces. Production increased in 2006 and 2007, but returned to negligible levels in 2008 and 2009.

In March 2007, a Marine convoy was attacked by a vehicle born improvised explosive device (VBIED) in eastern Nangarhar. A subsequent firefight killed an estimated 19 Afghan civilians, according to news reports. The incident eroded the trust between the population and the military.

In 2008, the population staged numerous protests against US forces' airstrikes and night arrests, which it blames for killing innocent civilians. Whether valid or not, these issues caused a fault line between the international community and the people.

Nangarharis have been supportive of the central government. However, in 2009, Nangarhar is a province caught between insurgents and the government and international community. The population feels somewhat betrayed by the president because it has drastically reduced poppy production and seen few rewards, while other provinces continue profiting from growing poppy without consequences. The insurgents have become bolder, planting IEDs and attempting to intimidate areas of the province that had been relatively safe. Frustration with authorities over corruption and the pace of development has led to mistrust and a lack of cooperation. The government's strong anti-poppy stance has alienated many farmers who are struggling for a better life, while watching corrupt government officials become rich. The Shinwari tribe, in particular, feels targeted by the government because it has the largest poppy-producing area and houses numerous processing labs.

*Tribal shuras are one of two mechanisms in which maliks (or tribal leaders) meet to make decisions. Their main focus is on redressing wrongs through arbitration or addressing issues of pride. The other mechanism is called a jirga, which is called to make a specific binding decision.*

PHOTO BY MICHELLE PARKER

# Chapter 2
# Ethnicity, Tribes,
# Languages, and Religion

## ETHNICITY

Pashtun is the dominant ethnic group in Nangarhar. Pashai are prevalent in the districts of Dari Nur and Koz Kunar on the northern tip of the province. The nomadic Kuchi spend much of their time in Nangarhar, especially in the winter, due to the mild climate. There are also small enclaves of Tajiks and Arabs, mostly around Jalalabad.

## ROLE OF TRIBES

The tribe is the most powerful structure of Pashtun society and provides an informal governance structure. Overarching decisions, such as allowing poppy cultivation, are usually made at the tribal level. Tribal society works on a group decision-making structure rather than an individual decision-making structure. All decisions for the tribe or sub-sections within a tribe are determined as a group by the tribal elders known as *maliks*. The goal of justice is to promote group harmony rather than punish an individual. However, the district sub-governors now are starting to resolve smaller community disputes at the district government level. Tribal influence also wanes closer to Jalalabad.

In Nangarhar, tribal boundaries are relatively stable, and conflict between tribes has been rare over the past few years. A Tribal Affairs Directorate oversees mitigation between tribes to keep this harmony. However, land disputes do pop up occasionally, especially where tribal boundaries meet or overlap. A current example of this is the new town being built near Hesarshahi in Rodat district along Highway 1. The government disagrees with the Mohmand tribe over whether the government or the tribe owns that stretch of land, and several people have been killed.

There are two primary mechanisms for tribal elders to make decisions. The first, a *jirga*, is a meeting held to make a specific decision. It can involve people from within or outside of the tribe. Any decision made in a jirga is considered binding. The other meeting type is called a *shura*, from the Arabic word for consultation. Shuras seek to redress wrongs through arbitration and address issues of pride and reparations more than they actually impose punishment. Shuras have become more militarized in Afghanistan after decades of war, acting as short-term advisory councils that can includes elders, commanders, and landowners.

## Prominent Tribes in Nangarhar

Located primarily in Chaparhar, Deh Bala, Achin, Shinwar, Bati Kot, Nazyan, and Dur Baba districts, the **Shinwari** consistently feud with the Khogiani. They are fiercely independent and have a history of opposing the central government. They are classified as Eastern or Sarbani Pashtuns. The Shinwari also allow opium production and heroin labs in their tribal areas, and smuggling is a major industry. Many of Nangarhar's primary smuggling routes cross Shinwari lands and are often the main entrance of insurgents from Pakistan. The Shinwari are well respected for their fighting. Rudyard Kipling wrote that you can never tame the heart of a Shinwari. It is as true today as it was then.

Located primarily in Sherzad, Khogiani, and Pachir Wa Agam districts, the **Khogiani** consistently feud within their own tribe and with other tribes. The Khogiani love to claim they fought harder than the other tribes against the British and Soviets. Most insurgent problems in Nangarhar are in the Khogiani tribal areas. Leaders such as Haji Zaman and Dr. Asif are Khogiani. This is the least united tribe in the province, as shown by their self-identification at the *khel*, or clan, level (Waziri, Sherzad, and Kharbone). Internal conflicts between the clans often lead to open fighting, making operations difficult for civilian relief organizations and the international military in their tribal area. They are classified as Karlanri and Hill Tribe Pashtuns.

Located primarily in Rodat, Kot, Bati Kot, Goshta, Behsood, Lalpur, Kama, and Momandara districts, **Mohmand** tribal areas are normally more peaceful than the Khogiani and Shinwari areas. The Mohmand are the most educated of all the tribes and tend to support the government policies. However, the Mohmand tribal areas along the border are more remote and are influenced by the Pakistani side, allowing insurgents an avenue into Nangarhar and Kunar. Mohmands tend to be supportive and hospitable to foreign aid workers. The Mohmand tribal areas push well into western Pakistan. They are classified as Eastern or Sarbani Pashtuns.

Located primarily in Dari Nur and Koz Kunar districts, **Pashai** inhabit northern Nangarhar, Laghman, and parts of Nuristan. Their native tongue is a Dardic language, a language group that extends to the foothills of the Hindu Kush. Nangarhar Pashais tend to be very hospitable to foreign aid workers and have benefited greatly from reconstruction efforts. They are also referred to as Kohistani (Kohistan is the name of two districts in Badakhshan, Afghanistan, and NWFP, Pakistan). They are occasionally referred to as *Shurrhi*, a derisive term for "hillbilly."

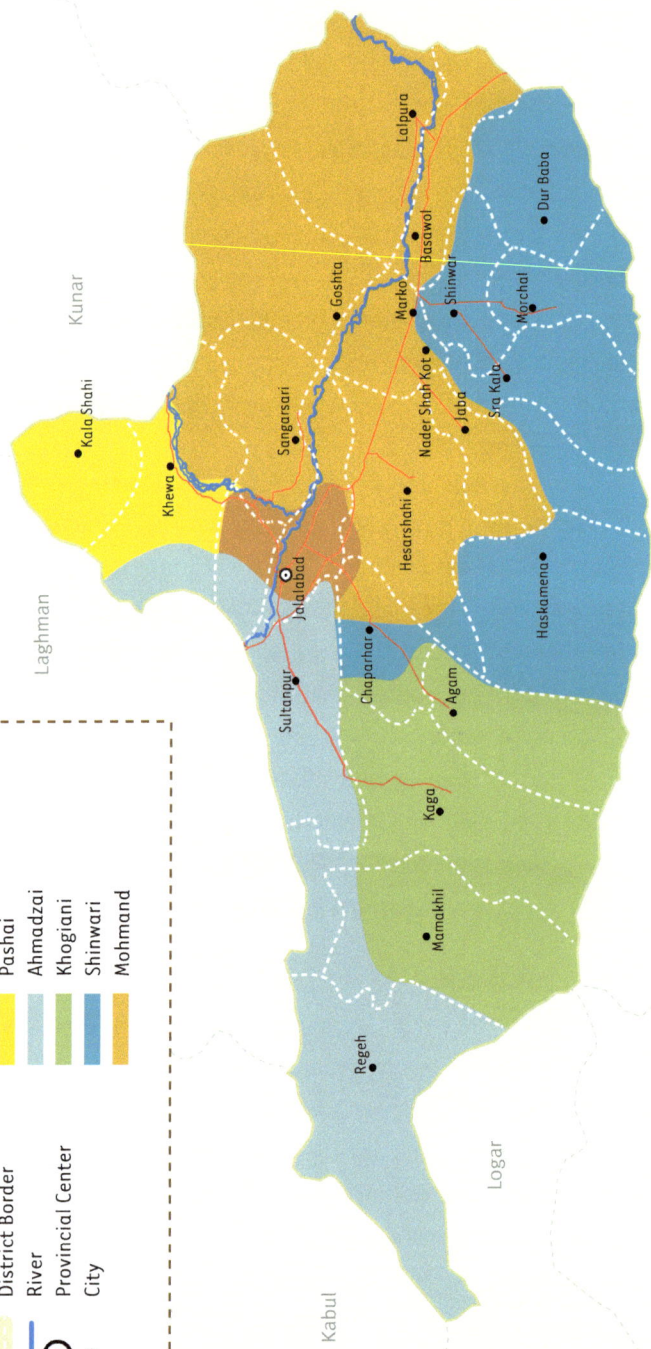

Map 2. Tribal Map of Nangarhar

Paved Road
District Border
River
Provincial Center
City

City Area – mixed
Pashai
Ahmadzai
Khogiani
Shinwari
Mohmand

Pakistan

Kunar

Laghman

Kabul

Logar

Paktya

Lalpura
Dur Baba
Basawol
Goshta
Markoh
Shinwa
Morchal
Sangarsari
Nader Shah Kot
Jaba
Sra Kala
Kala Shahi
Khewa
Hesarshahi
Haskamena
Jalalabad
Sultanpur
Chaparhar
Agam
Kaga
Mamakhil
Regeh

Located primarily in Hesarak and Surkh Rod districts, the **Ahmadzai** in Surkh Rod have benefited greatly from their close proximity to Jalalabad and have worked well with the international community. The Ahmadzai in Hesarak are among the most isolated people in the province. They are known for growing vast amounts of hashish but are a relatively peaceful people. The former governor, Haji Din Mohamad, and former border police chief, Haji Zahir, are the most important members of this tribe. When Governor Sherzai assumed the governorship, he began to erode the Ahmadzai's power by replacing most Ahmadzais in high level positions. The Ahmadzai still have considerable sway with the people of Nangarhar.

## Other Ethnic Groups

Although the **Kuchi** in Nangarhar are mainly Pashtun, they are a nomadic people who tend to migrate throughout the provinces. They camp in open areas and normally deal in livestock. Due to harsh winters in most Afghan provinces, many Kuchi migrate to Nangarhar, where winters are milder. Kuchi often set up camp in Surkh Rod, Chaparhar, Behsood, and Jalalabad districts.

The **Sikhs** in Nangarhar account for less than one percent of the population. They are not Hindus but come from areas in northern India and have similar customs to Hindus. They are found mostly around Jalalabad and surrounding districts.

There are a few villages in Nangarhar that are made up of **ethnic Arabs** who have migrated to the region over the centuries. They make up around two percent of the population. They typically have a slight accent when they speak Pashto.

**Tajiks** make up less than two percent of the population in Nangarhar. They live mostly in Jalalabad and surrounding areas. They normally speak Dari.

## LANGUAGES

Pashto is the primary language in Nangarhar, although the districts of
Dari Nur and part of Koz Kunar (Khewa) speak Pashai as well. Many
people also speak Dari, but speaking Dari or producing literature in Dari
is frowned upon. Urdu is spoken among those whose families moved
to Pakistan during the Soviet-Afghan war. Some of the older population
speak Russian. English is now taught in schools, and children enjoy
using their basic English phrases with foreigners.

## THE ROLE OF RELIGION

Islam is very important to the culture of most Afghans in Nangarhar.
Even if a person is not truly pious, he will at least appear to be, and
it would be unwise to challenge that. No outsider should ever speak
poorly about Islam or accuse an Afghan of being un-Islamic. It is good
to compliment someone for being a good Muslim, but the topic of
religion should be approached lightly, if at all.

Mullahs have a special place of influence over the people. Because
Afghanistan is an Islamic Republic, there is no separation between religion
and government. All laws must be in line with Islamic principles. The
Director of Religious Affairs (often called Director of Haj) is the government's official representative for the mullah community in the province.
He has significant influence over the mullahs throughout the districts.
There is a network of mullahs that is run through the director's office in
Jalalabad. Each district has several mullahs that often come to Jalalabad
to represent the communities of their districts. Messages are coordinated
through the director's office to influence the mullahs throughout the
province. The current director is interested in doing what is best for the
Muslim community and is open to speaking with military commanders
to find peaceful solutions to problems. He will assist commanders in

communicating with mullahs or set up large gatherings where the military can engage directly with the mullahs. Consistent engagements with the mullah community through the Director of Haj has proven to be one of the best ways to win the support of the religious community and get messages to the population through Friday prayers.

## Relevant Cultural Points – Beliefs, Prejudices, and Behaviors

Afghans are a very proud people. Although they are accepting of outsiders when it benefits them, there is always a feeling of mistrust. Throughout recent history, many conquering armies and unstable governments have come and gone, always promising stability, security, and economic development. Very few of these promises have been kept. Corruption and a "me first" mentality loom as stability has decreased. Afghans do not appreciate it when people raise their voices and openly fight or swear. It is rare to see two Afghans yelling at each other for an extended time in meetings. Normally, when an Afghan wants to make a strong point, he will raise his voice and not be challenged by anyone else raising their voice. Patience is important when meeting with Afghans. Consensus is important when meeting with a shura, and everyone needs a chance to speak. Often meetings will end with no resolution, and this is often fine with Afghans.

Respect and honor are very important to Afghans. Always act respect-fully by shaking hands with everyone when you enter a room. Even when a group is already meeting, it is customary for new arrivals to interrupt the meeting to shake hands with everyone. Afghans do not consider this rude, but normal. When shaking hands with someone, always use the right hand and then place your hand directly on your heart as a sign of respect. If you are able to, take off your shoes when entering a room if others have done so. Normally, the host will tell you not to take them off, but it is polite to offer.

*Many attribute Nangarhar's stability to its governor, Gul Agha Sherzai, who is influential both provincially and nationally. He has also been accused of corruption, both from his time as governor of Kandahar and illegal tolls he charges on freight passing through Torkham Gate.*

PHOTO BY CAPT. DUSTIN HART

# Chapter 3
# Government and Leadership

Nangarhar has a stronger government than most provinces, featuring an influential provincial governor and effective central government administration. Parliament members represent their populations in the central government in Kabul, but rarely come back to the province. Governor Sherzai is quite powerful and has some influence over the selection of line directors. The primary governance challenges are rivalries between the governor and ministry officials, customs and corruption issues, and influence in the outlying areas.

## HOW THE GOVERNMENT OFFICIALLY WORKS

### Central Control

Authority and power in Afghanistan are concentrated in the national government as a means to counter the power of warlords in the provinces. As such, the provincial government is limited to an advisory role for the central government, while decisions on everything from policy to funding priorities are made in Kabul.

## Provincial Government

A governor (*wali*) heads the provincial government and reports to the Independent Directorate for Local Governance (IDLG) located in the Executive Office of the President. A deputy and several staff that oversee provincial government management assist him. Ministries in Kabul execute their policies and programs through departments located at the provincial level. Ministers, with the approval of the president, appoint provincial directors who manage the departments. The director reports to and receives funds from the ministry in Kabul. The governor does not have budgetary authority over any of these departments, but must approve all expenditures before they are processed by the Department of Finance (*Mustafiat*).

The Provincial Council (PC) is the only elected body at the provincial level. It provides a voice for the people in advising on provincial issues. The PC reports directly to the president and has no budget. Its relevance is largely dependent on the governor's support and on its members' individual resources and ambitions.

The Provincial Development Committee (PDC), including the governor and department heads, is responsible for creating the Provincial Development Plan (PDP) and coordinating with key players on development needs. External players such as the UN, PRT, and interested NGOs also attend meetings.

## District and Local Governance

Government at the district level mirrors the provincial government with the *woluswal* (district administrator or sub-governor), police chief, National Directorate of Security officer, clerks, and a small police force. Ministry sub-departments also operate at the district level, but are not present in every district. In 2007, District Development Assemblies

(DDAs) were formed in order to plan, prioritize, and coordinate development activities at the district level. Below the district level, the only formal governance structures are the Community Development Councils (CDCs). These CDCs help MRRD manage the National Solidarity Program. The municipality of Jalalabad is led by a mayor appointed by the president in consultation with the governor. Municipalities are independent from the provincial government and are free to plan, fund, and implement projects, as well as tax local businesses.

## HOW IT ACTUALLY WORKS

Government in Nangarhar works extraordinarily well compared to most Afghan provinces. All of the critical positions are filled, mostly with competent people who do a decent job. The government's influence can be felt in areas near Jalalabad or along Highway 1. In the more remote parts of the province, tribal influence is more strongly felt than government influence. In general, the provincial administration is aware of and follows the central government policies. The internal dynamics between the governor and the directors is improving. However, most would agree that the governor has considerably more influence over money and development projects than he rightfully should.

### Provincial Government

Governor Sherzai, through force of personality and reputation, asserts his authority over many aspects of Nangarhar's administration. Government staff generally support his leadership, although power struggles among directors sometimes prevent close cooperation. Very few decisions are made without the governor's approval or input. Kabul usually does not interfere with Governor Sherzai's management because the province is relatively stable and flourishing economically. Many tribal leaders dislike Sherzai and much political posturing is expected to occur among parties and tribes to get their preferred candidate appointed governor in the event that Sherzai leaves.

As a general rule, the line departments that have good leadership from Kabul tend to withstand the governor's interference better than those with weak leadership. Some examples of strong departments are: Rural Rehabilitation and Development, Public Health, Finance, Judiciary, Agriculture, Public Works, and the Cadastre office. Some examples of weak departments are: Power, Irrigation, Municipalities, and Haj and Islamic Affairs.

## Provincial Council

The PC works better in Nangarhar than PCs in most provinces. Governor Sherzai supports it by providing salaries, office space, and transportation for the members. The head of the PC, Fazel Hadi Muslimyar, is very active in the province and is usually by Governor Sherzai's side at public events to show government unity. The members of the PC take their jobs seriously and advocate on behalf of their citizens as best they can, given the constraints. The four PCs of the Eastern Region meet occasionally in Jalalabad and unofficially elected Muslimyar as the head of the eastern PCs in 2005. In Nangarhar, one of the PC members, Qazi Khan Mohmmad from Dari Nur district, was assassinated. Although the Taliban claims responsibility, two of the assassins were captured after the attack on the land of former Laghman police chief and known warlord, Gul Karim. The attackers were executed on site by the local villagers who claim the attackers confessed that Gul Karim was the organizer of the attack. Despite protests, no action has been taken against Gul Karim. The motive behind the attack may have been to replace the slain elected official with someone under the influence of Gul Karim in the future PC elections.

The Provincial Coordination Center (PCC) is staffed with liaison officers from each Afghan and ISAF element in the province. If and when a crisis erupts, security forces are able to coordinate and make decisions together.

## District and Local-level Government

The district sub-governors are beginning to show more authority and are becoming key to solving problems and managing systems and development at the district level. This increased activity will help bring communities away from traditional tribal structures and take a more active role in the government. The advent of District Development Assemblies (DDAs) in each district has helped bridge the development gap between the provincial government and PRTs and the local communities, ensuring that priority projects get more attention than individual requests.

In more remote areas, traditional tribal shuras are still the main authority. These informal bodies dispense justice, mediate conflicts, and raise militias *(arbakai)* if they feel threatened. The key decision makers can be a group consisting of any combination of the following: tribal elders *(maliks)*, land owners *(khans)*, religious leaders *(mullahs)*, and water managers *(mirabs)*. The types of issues resolved at this level include small legal disputes, small fights, petty theft, etc. The community tries to resolve significant legal issues, such as murder, a large land dispute, or organized crime. If they cannot, the issue will be referred to the formal legal system.

## Tribal and Traditional Structures

In Afghanistan, traditional organizations based on tribe, culture, and religion are often the most legitimate and effective local governance bodies available. The dynamics are shifting as the provincial government attempts to reach out to maliks and mullahs. Some traditional leaders are being incorporated into the official government, but others are resisting these overtures. Afghans, especially those outside of urban areas, make decisions as a group, and the leaders are responsible for discussing those decisions and reaching consensus.

## Corruption

Corruption is common in Nangarhar's government. Officials taking bribes and funneling off money for themselves or their leaders mar nearly every program and revenue generation vehicle. However, it is difficult to prove specific incidents of corruption because no one will publicly charge another individual.

## SECURITY FORCES

## Afghan Border Police (ABP)

The regional ABP headquarters for the Eastern Region is in Jalalabad with posts in Ghosta, Lalpur, Dur Baba, Ghanikhel, and Torkham. The ABP is still considered corrupt. ABP posts in the mountain passes are a recurring target of the insurgents. A new mentoring program has begun to help train the ABP using US government contractors, but it is not known at this time how effective the program is.

## Afghan National Army (ANA)

The ANA has become the most trusted security agency in Afghanistan, and the troops are not afraid to fight for their country. There are two ANA bases in Nangarhar: one adjacent to the PRT and one stationed on the main highway in Rodat. With consistent training, the ANA eventually will be able take over full security roles in Afghanistan.

## Afghan National Police (ANP)

The ANP is relatively respected by the local population in most districts. However, corruption remains a constant problem. A consistent mentoring program and a recent influx of funding and equipment have helped their capabilities. The police are more respected and effective closer to Jalalabad, but have much less influence in the outer districts where tribal structures are more effective.

## National Directorate for Security (NDS)

The Afghan intelligence service, NDS, is made up of highly educated officers. Many were trained during the communist regime and are generally not trusted by the local population. They seem to be relatively effective in Nangarhar and have thwarted several terrorist attempts.

## POLITICAL PARTIES

## Hezb-e Afghan Millat (Afghan National Party)

This Pashtun party is led by Finance Minister Dr. Anwar Ul-haq Ahadi. The party has over 11,000 members in Nangarhar. It maintains a muted, ethno-nationalist rhetoric focused on unity, security, and an Islamic version of democracy.

## Hezb-e Islami

This party is now re-established under the leadership of Haji Stoaray. Although no longer officially part of HIG or HIK, many of its members are still the same. This party is still influential in Nangarhar, with members such as General Ghafar, former police chief; Qari Dilaqa, vice chancellor of Nangarhar University; and other influential people.

## Ittehad-e Islami Afghanistan

Founded by Professor Abdurbrasul Sayaf, this party has support from Arab countries. Nangarhar PC Chair, Fazal Hadi Muslimyar, is an active member.

## Jabha-e Meli Nejat Afghanistan (National Liberation Front)

Led by Sibghatullah Mujadiddi, former president of Afghanistan, the party's platform includes the goal of a peaceful Islamic democracy in Afghanistan. Haji Hayet Khan, director of martyrs, disabled, and social work, is the representative in Nangarhar.

## Peace Caravan

Led by former border police chief and influential warlord, Haji Zahir, this organization started operations in 2007 as a social organization to promote peace and security across the borders between Nangarhar and the FATA. Not officially a political party but warrants mentioning here due to its political influence.

## 2009 ELECTIONS

Presidential and Provincial Council elections are scheduled to take place 20 August 2009. When President Karzai's term expired in May, he began serving as a caretaker president until elections could be held. Candidates for president filed in May, but few national contenders emerged, as President Karzai persuaded many of his rivals not to challenge him. In terms of security, Afghan National Security Forces (ANSF) will be extensively involved in the elections, recruiting 23,000 police and soldiers for the event.

The security of the elections represents a potential key moment for the summer fighting season between Taliban and ANSF/ISAF troops. After the elections, the changes in the Afghan government will include new senior appointments, including new ministers and governors. Late 2009 and 2010 will be a key period for these new officials to leverage their public mandate and expand international assistance to deliver more accountable and credible governance to the Afghan people.

A more detailed update on elections is included in the back folder of your book or can be downloaded at *www.idsinternational.net/afpakbooks*. The pre-elections update goes into the elections process in greater detail and the post-election update will summarize the results and implications.

## LEADER PROFILES

**Gul Agha Sherzai, Governor:** Gul Agha Sherzai, about 55 years old, is a Barakzai Pashtun from Kandahar, and has served as Nangarhar governor since June 2005. He is politically affiliated with the Mahaz-e Milli Islami party. Sherzai recaptured Kandahar from the Taliban within hours of the Northern Alliance victory in Kabul in 2001. He was

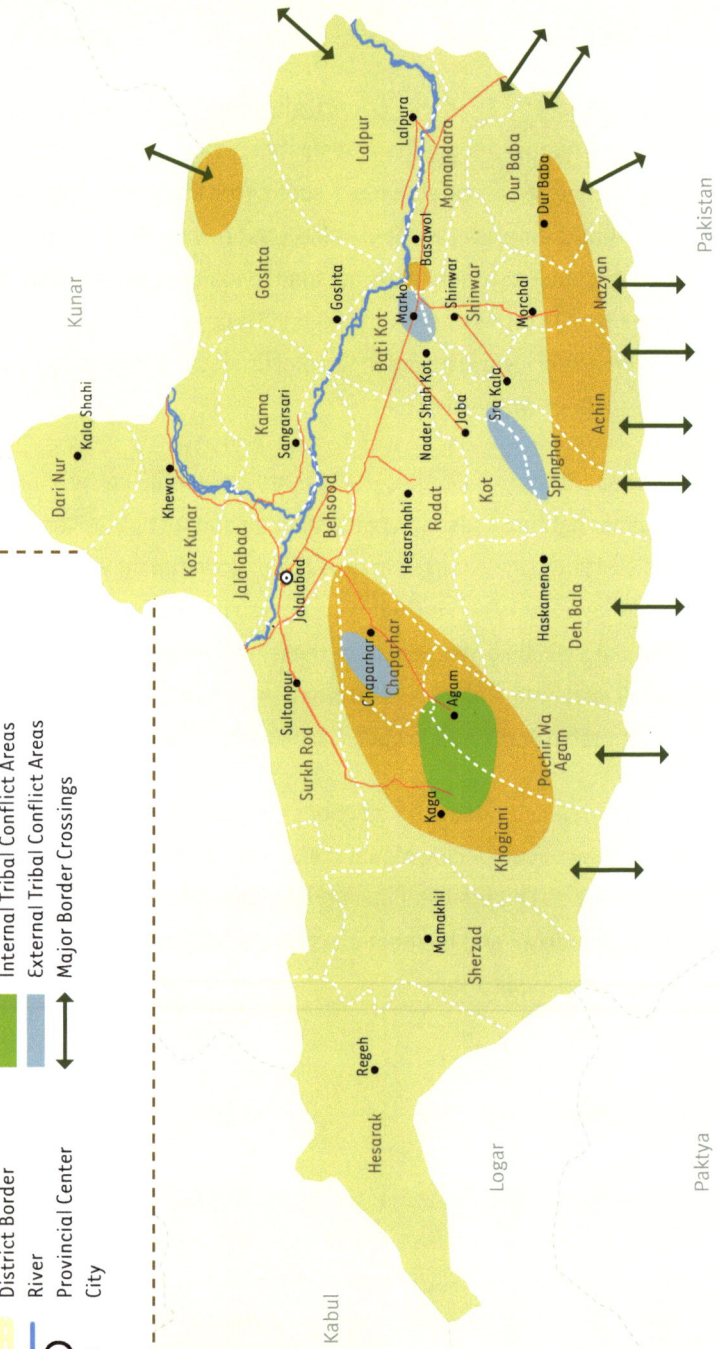

# Map 3. Conflict Map of Nangarhar

**Paved Road**
**District Border**
**River**
**Provincial Center**
**City**

**Areas of Anti-Government Tribal Violence**
**Internal Tribal Conflict Areas**
**External Tribal Conflict Areas**
**Major Border Crossings**

Kunar

Pakistan

Lalpur
Lalpura
Momandara
Dur Baba
Dur Baba
Goshta
Goshta
Basawol
Bati Kot
Marko
Shinwar
Shinwar
Morchal
Nazyan
Kama
Sangarsari
Nader Shah Kot
Jaba
Sra Kala
Achin
Spinghar
Kala Shahi
Dari Nur
Khewa
Koz Kunar
Behsood
Hesarshahi
Rodat
Kot
Jalalabad
Jalalabad
Sultanpur
Chaparhar
Chaparhar
Agam
Haskamena
Deh Bala
Surkh Rod
Kaga
Pachir Wa Agam
Khogiani
Mamakhil
Sherzad
Regeh
Kabul
Hesarak
Logar
Paktya

appointed governor of Kandahar and held the symbolic position of minister adviser to President Karzai.

As a successful governor and a member of one of the more influential tribes, Sherzai was rumored to be considering running for president in 2009. Most independent observers felt that his reputation for corruption and his lack of support outside the Pashtun community would have doomed his candidacy. However, he would probably have siphoned enough votes from President Karzai to endanger his re-election. In May of 2009, Sherzai met with the president and shortly thereafter stated he would not be a candidate. This will significantly strengthen Karzai's chances. It has also almost certainly earned Sherzai political points with the president. There is speculation he will seek a ministerial position, possibly Interior, in the next administration.

While serving in Kandahar, Sherzai was accused of corruption and was transferred to Nangarhar. He still has strong family, ethnic, and business ties to Kandahar. His inner circle in Nangarhar is primarily made up of Kandarharis. Sherzai has vigorously opposed poppy production since coming to Nangarhar. He has narrowly escaped at least three assassination attempts. Sherzai has a very aggressive and confrontational style, but he accomplishes his priorities. He deserves credit for his reconstruction efforts in the provincial capital of Jalalabad, but has done little outside the city. Many projects are awarded to companies in which he has an interest, and he routinely fails to follow legal procedures or to integrate plans with international donors or other local officials. Much of his reconstruction money appears to come from illegal tolls charged on freight entering via Torkham Gate. Sherzai has shared his ambition to become a major minister or possibly president some day. He has three wives, 17 children, and a few grandchildren. He speaks Pashto, some Dari, and understands very limited English. Recently, he has been targeted by the attorney general for corruption, but there is no official report on the outcome of this investigation.

**LTG Mohammad Ayoub Salangi, Police Chief:** LTG Salangi was moved to Nangarhar province in March 2009. He is a Sunni Pashtun and was a commander in the Northern Alliance. He is affiliated with HIG and has strong political connections to former Minister of the Interior Parwan and Member of Parliament Haji Almas. His police experience includes Kandahar chief of police (March-July 2005), Herat chief of police (July 2005-December 2006), Kunduz chief of police (2007), and a position in the criminal investigation division in Kabul.

**Fazal Hadi Muslimyar, Provincial Council Chairman:** Born around 1972, Muslimyar is originally from Daouladze village in Chaparhar district. He is a protégé of former Nangarhar Police Chief Malingyar. He often serves as a mediator in disputes between the PRT and local leaders. He is rumored to have formerly been associated with the Taliban's Abu Amer Bel Maroof and Nahi Anil Munkhar (Ministry of the Promotion of Virtue and Punishment of Vice). He lost three brothers in the fight against the Soviets. He was implicated in a corruption case involving the sale of government land at Hada Farms. His relationship with Sherzai is strained, but they appear to have reached a truce. He apparently speaks several languages, including Arabic. He does not speak English, but understands some. He has very close relations with President Karzai.

**Hazrat Ali, Member of Parliament:** Currently a Pashai member of parliament from Kashmond village, Dari Nur district, Hazrat Ali was a junior commander of HIK during the Soviet occupation. He then became a member of the Northern Alliance. The US Special Forces chose to partner with Ali when taking back Jalalabad. He took part in the battle of Tora Bora and is sometimes blamed for allowing al-Qaeda members, including Osama bin Laden, to escape. Through US support, Hazrat Ali rose to prominence in Nangarhar. He was the first commander to take control of Jalalabad, and he declared himself governor. Karzai's interim government, however, appointed Hazrat Ali as the head of the Eastern Region Army Garrison. He later served as Nangarhar chief of police. In May 2008, his father was murdered and seven of his family members were kidnapped from his home in Dari Nur.

**Hadji Din Mohammed:** Former governor of Nangarhar province until June 2005, Hadji Din Mohammed was transferred to the governorship of Kabul province. He belongs to the Arsala family, which maintained political leadership of Nangarhar from 1992-2005, with the exception of the Taliban era. His brothers are Haji Abdul Qadir (former governor and vice president, assassinated 2002), Abdul Haq (former mujahedin commander, assassinated 2001), and Haji Baryalai (stayed in Germany during the war years, and returned after the Taliban left to run the Abdul Haq Foundation, a civil-society NGO). He is the uncle of Haji Zahir, former chief of the border police (see below). He frequently returns to Nangarhar where he still has political influence. He maintains a house in Jalalabad city near UNAMA headquarters.

**Hadji Zahir:** Son of the assassinated former Vice President Hadji Qadir and nephew of assassinated mujahedin commander Abdul Haq and Kabul Governor Hadji Din Mohammed, Hadji Zahir was the Regional Border Commander for Nangarhar, Kunar, and Nuristan from 2002-2007. In 2007, he was reassigned to Takhar province. He is in his 30s and has accumulated a vast amount of wealth and power. He has a large family compound in Surkh Rod district where Abdul Haq is buried. In 2007, he was implicated in a heroin smuggling operation, but was never charged. He started a new organization, Peace Caravan, in 2007, in an attempt to regain political influence in Nangarhar.

**Table 2.** Nangarhar Provincial Line Directors and Government Officials

| TITLE OF DUTY | NAME | PHONE NUMBER |
|---|---|---|
| Governor | Gul Agha Shirzai | N/A |
| Deputy Governor | Dr. Mohammad Alam Ishaqzai | 0798-555-558 0700-202-307 |
| Chief Executive Director | Mohammad Hanif Gardewal | 0700-271-393 0799-196-581 |
| Director of Administration | Malik Nazir | 0799-348-339 0700-604-685 |
| Chief of Staff of Governor | Masood Azizi | 0700-329-596 |
| Director of Education | Mohammad Iqbal "Azizi" | 0799-876-441 |
| Director of Nangarhar High Court | Ziaulhaq Denarzai | 0700-200-055 |
| Director of Agriculture | Mohammad Hussain "Safai" | 0799-395-465 |
| Director of Canal "NVDA" | Eng. M Hakim | 0700-600-080 |
| Provincial Prosecutor | Abdul Qayum | 0700-604-134 |
| Director of Customs | Ehsanullah "Kamawal" | 0700-601-417 070-278-582 |
| Chancellor of Nangarhar University | Amanullah "Hamidzai" | 0799-067-555 0700-640-460 |
| Nangarhar Province Mayor | Lal Agha "Kakar" | 0700-017-587 0799-569-191 |
| Director of Culture and Information | Aurang "Samim" | 0700-603-576 |
| Director of Energy and Power | Eng. Redi Gul | 0799-181-291 0756-001-641 |
| Director of RRD | Eng. Ahmad Wali | 070-292-026 070-487-714 |
| Director of Urban Development | Eng. Zakheel | 070-605-399 |

| TITLE OF DUTY | NAME | PHONE NUMBER |
|---|---|---|
| Director of Public Works | Eng. Arif | 0700-604-693 |
| Director of Irrigation | Delawar Khan | 0700-601-586<br>0797-050-277 |
| Director of Haj & Awqaf | Mawlavi Asadullah "Sajid" | 0700-607-800 |
| Director of Women's Affairs | Sheela Baburi | 0700-629-514 |
| General Director of Finance | Dr. M. Alam. Ishaqzai | 0799-202-307 |
| Director of Economy | Sayed Qayas "Saeedi" | 070-607-766<br>0777-668-646 |
| Director of Public Health | Ajmal "Pardis" | 0799-096-576<br>070-601-088 |
| Director of Government Cases | Mahmood Khalil | 070-365-293 |
| Director of Refugees & Returnees | Abdur Rahman "Shams" | 070-602-364<br>070-159-140 |
| Rep. of Foreign Affairs | Wahid Azizi | 0786-422-322 |
| Director of Red Cross | Mohammad Iqbal "Said" | 0700-631-585<br>0799-373-859 |
| Head of Youth Affairs | Noor Agha "Zwak" | 0700-607-089 |
| Director of Narcotics | Mohammad Yaqoub | 0797-419-786 |
| Director of NDR | Addul Wahab Sherzad | 079-346-782 |
| Director of Chamber of Commerce | Haji Noor Agha | 0700-603-557 |
| Director of Communication | Abdur Razzaq "Saqib" | 070-221-769 |
| Director of Admin. Reform (Acting) | Ghulam Ali Joshan | 0799-202-162 |

| TITLE OF DUTY | NAME | PHONE NUMBER |
|---|---|---|
| Director of Water Supply | Said Rahman | 0700-634-345 0799-241-508 |
| Director of Monopolies | Said Ahmad Shah | 070-600-094 |
| Director of Human Rights & Claims | M. Naeem Durani | 0799-171-418 |
| Director of Children's Ed. | Sadaqat Kotwal | N/A |
| Director of Transport | Khan Wazir | N/A |
| Director of National Bus (Milli Bus) | Mohammad Gulab | 0799-012-376 |
| Director of Sports | Sayed Alam | 0700-607-645 |
| Director of Tribal Affairs | Dr. Ayoub Sharafat | 0777-611-034 |
| Head of Nangarhar Radio and TV | Eng. Zalmai | 0799-407-372 |
| Director of Social Affairs, Martyrs & Disabled | Haji Hayat Khan | 0799-405-928 070-601-171 |
| Director of Mines & Industries | Eng. Abdullah | 070-630-297 |
| Director of Da Afghanistan Bank | Haji Rohullah | N/A |
| Chief of Police | LTG Mohammad Ayoub Salangi | 0700-273-333 |
| Chief of Border Police | Qadir Gul (Deputy of ABP) | 0799-328-668 0700-623-177 |
| Director of Security | Chief of Bureau | 070-634-795 0799-331-692 |
| National Security | General Abdul Sabor | 0799-079-945 |
| Spokesman of Governor | Abdulzai | N/A |

## Table 3. Nangarhar District Sub-governors

| NAME | FATHER'S NAME | DISTRICT NAME | CONTACT NUMBERS |
|---|---|---|---|
| Hazrat Khan | Zaman Begh | Shinwar | 0700-606-150 0799-274-754 |
| Ghulam Farooq Himat | Mohammad Yousof | Khogiani | 0774-296-090 0799-593-281 |
| Mohammad Turab | Mir Salam | Surkh Rod | 0700-604-630 0774-477-926 |
| Khorsaid | Haji Mohammad Younus | Rodat | 0799-466-060 |
| Isa Khan "Zwak" | Aqa Mohammad | Goshta | 0700-602-022 |
| Abdul Wahab | Wali Jan | Achin | 0799-366-468 |
| Eng. Shukrullah Durani | Abdul Satar | Behsood | 0700-604-219 0777-604-522 |
| Haji Abdul Qayum | Haji Mohammad Naeem | Dur Baba | 0775-744-843 |
| Azizullah Shinwari | Mohammad Yousof | Koz Kunar | 0799-197-240 |
| Haji Abdullah | Dilawar Khan | Pachir Wa Agam | 0798-216-491 0700-616-550 |
| Hassan Khan | Zabta Khan | Chaparhar | 0799-287-203 0700-610-098 |
| Said Ali Akbar | Said Ali Asghar | Kama | 0700-190-314 0777-393-804 |
| Said Mohammad | Malik Mohammad Jan | Nazyan | 0799-331-839 |
| Khyber Khan | Aminullah Khan | Bati Kot | 0799-454-970 |
| Abdul Haq | Mohammad Usman | Kot | 0799-175-233 |
| Hamisha Gul | Ajab Gul | Deh Bala | 0799-171-701 |
| Masooq Khan | Shah Ghasie | Dari Nur | 0700-633-264 |
| Mirza Mohammad | Painda Mohammad | Lalpur | 0777-611-920 |
| Zalmai | Haji Said Alam | Momandara | 0799-364-287 |
| Mamur Essa | Gull Forosh | Hesarak | 0799-816-925 |
| Haji Said Rahman | N/A | Sherzad | N/A |
| Jandul | N/A | Spinghar | 0700-604-643 077-478-650 |

*Nangarhar's rural population depends on agriculture. Sixty-seven percent of farming is subsistance, with less than one percent of farmers exporting their crops for sale. Some subsistance farmers sell their surplus in local markets, but the agricultural sector remains rudimentary due to outdated practices, poor roads, and no lending establishments.*

PHOTO BY MICHELLE PARKER

# Chapter 4
# The Economy

Relative to the rest of Afghanistan, Nangarhar's economy is doing well. It boasts one of the highest employment rates in Afghanistan, with 35 percent employment. Nangarhar possesses an efficient credit system within Afghanistan's nascent commercial banking sector, though borrowing is still difficult. Opium is also used as currency in the rural areas, as it is easily stored and holds its value relatively well. However, since the poppy ban has been enforced more strictly over the past two years, opium has lost its luster as a currency.

The formal currency in Afghanistan is the afghani, which has traded at roughly 50 to $1 since its introduction in 2002. In Nangarhar, however, the Pakistani rupee is often used in the markets. The government has tried to prohibit the use of other currency in the country, but cannot enforce any such policy. Nangarharis will also accept US dollars and euros, but they are not used in day-to-day market activities.

Another economic boost is the ability of Nangarhar residents to work in Pakistan. Many extended families have only one or two breadwinners who support the entire family with one job, and many of them work in Pakistan and send money home.

# KEY ECONOMIC SECTORS

## Agriculture

Most people outside of Jalalabad rely on agriculture for their livelihood. Farmers are broken into three categories: commercial, surplus, and subsistence. Commercial farmers that are able to sell crops for export make up less than one percent of all farmers. Surplus farmers make up 33 percent and both farm for subsistence and sell off a part of their crop locally. Subsistence farmers make up 67 percent and farm mostly food for their families.

Although there is plenty of arable land, irrigation systems are critical and in disrepair. Other hindrances to rebuilding the agricultural industry include outdated farming practices, limited veterinary services, poor roads, lack of storage or processing plants, few lending establishments for farmers, and poor seed quality. The USAID Alternative Development Program/Eastern Region (ADP/ER), the military's Agribusiness Development Team (ADT), and several relief organizations are attempting to build a solid agribusiness sector utilizing higher value crops and marketing techniques to increase income to farmers.

## Marble Production

The southern and western mountainous regions of Nangarhar have vast deposits of marble. There are at least ten small marble factories in Nangarhar, mostly on the outskirts of Jalalabad. Marble is typically extracted using unexploded ordnance, which destroys roughly 80 percent of the mineral. The marble factories cut the stone into slabs and small chips used for flooring, but lack the ability to sculpt the marble into other useable products. USAID's Afghan Small and Medium Enterprise Development (ASMED) program is working with companies to use modern cutting equipment to quarry the stone to an exportable quality, adding value with minimal losses. The marble factory owners, though, claim that the largest challenges to growing their business are the illegal checkpoints between Jalalabad and Kabul, where they must bribe their way to larger markets.

## TRENDS AND RELEVANT ISSUES

### *Future Potential*

If security in Nangarhar continues to improve, the economic future for Nangarhar is encouraging. The Afghanistan Investment Services Association (AISA) is working with investors to set up a 200-hectare industrial park on the main Jalalabad-Pakistan highway, funded by a $25 million grant from the World Bank. AISA hopes to provide 11 MW of electricity and water systems to the industrial park residents. The park will house agriculture processing, plastic and paper recycling, cotton and textiles, carpet, marble, and other businesses.

The substantial rise in crop prices over the past two years has been both a help and hindrance to rural Nangarharis. Increased prices, along with a decline in opium prices and stricter law enforcement, have helped convince some farmers to stop poppy cultivation. On the other hand, the higher price of wheat and rice, staples of the Afghan diet, have also caused poor families to go with less. Rural families

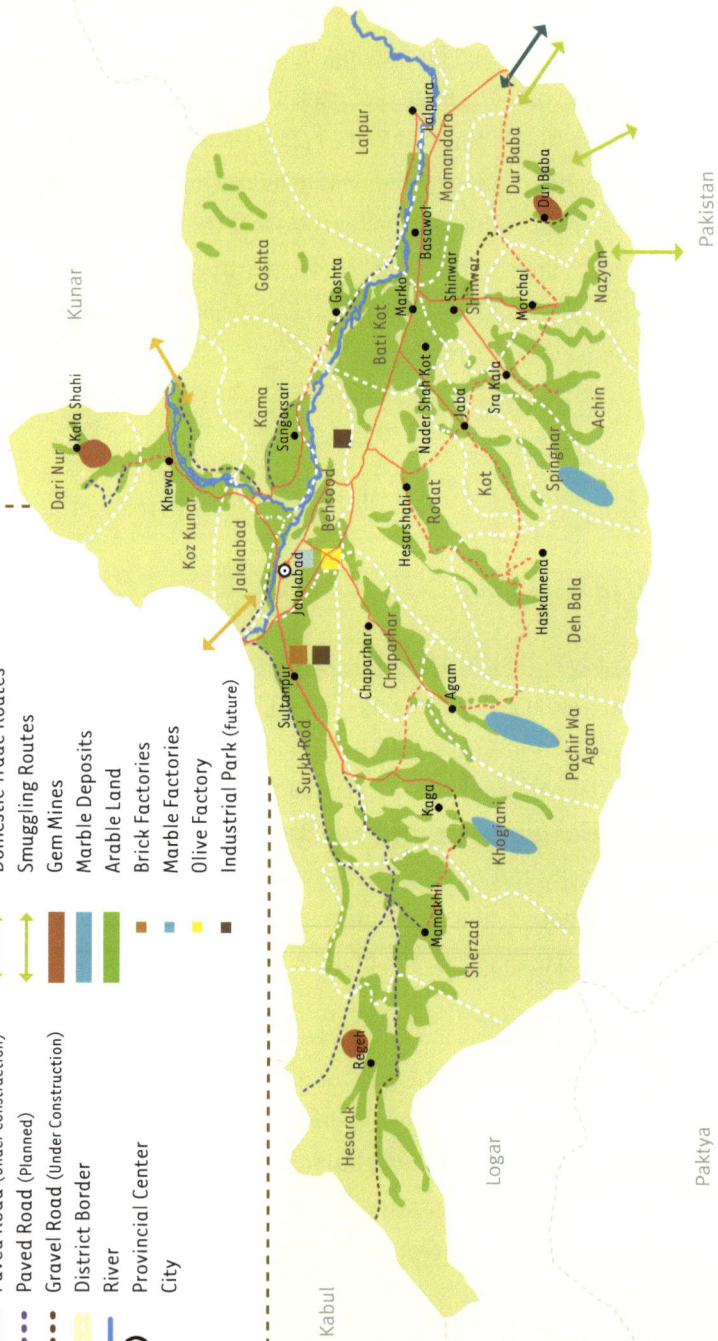

Map 4. Economic Map of Nangarhar

expressed their anger over food prices in several protests to the government in 2008-2009.

## *Obstacles*

Cheap and reliable power is needed in order to create factories and increase employment. When Darunta and the Naglu Dams are complete (see Ch 5), some of these problems may be mitigated. Nangarhar lacks the skilled workers to operate factory equipment. Government tax incentives and contract law are not in place to attract investors. Pakistan and Iran are less than cooperative when it comes to easing Afghanistan's access to ports. Cargo can remain in port for a month before being shipped to Afghanistan, with multiple bribes required just to get materials transferred across borders. These problems are compounded by the instability of Pakistan's FATA region.

The Moqam Khan siphon was installed as part of a PRT-funded project to repair Nangarhar's Grand Kanal. Costing roughly $2.8 million, the project involved the repair of 850 gates and installation of five new siphons. The irrigation system of the province depends upon such canals and karezes to feed crops. Unfortunately, most are still in need of repair or rebuilding.

PHOTO BY CAPT. DUSTIN HART

# Chapter 5
## Reconstruction Activities and International Organizations

## KEY ISSUES AND ACTIVITIES

### Electricity

An average 19 percent of households in Nangarhar province have access to electricity. Access to electricity is much greater in urban areas, where 83 percent of households can get intermittent power. However, this figure falls to just nine percent in rural areas.

Jalalabad is the only city with a power grid and significant generation. Darunta Dam, which is under construction, currently produces between 3-6 MW of power, but is forecast to output 11 MW when complete by the end of 2010. This power is intermittent and does not satisfy the demand. The grid is also quite archaic, with constant failures, but there is an upgrade plan. Another 20 MW will be coming to Jalalabad in 2010-2011 from the Naglu Dam near Surobi.

There are plans for hydropower dams on the Kunar River, which could produce enough power to meet commercial and residential needs. There is also potential for microhydro power in the outer districts. It is estimated that there are over 300 possible locations for 5-100 kW systems to handle the power needs of individual communities.

## Transportation

Roads will remain one of the top priorities in the near future. Since 2005, the Roads Technical Working Group has prioritized and streamlined the building of the major road systems. The priority is to complete the paving of all major roads linking district centers to Jalalabad and then to connect district centers along the southern mountains. The building of these paved roads has cut travel time in half through the province.

## Irrigation

Irrigation is another important sector. More than 80 percent of the population outside of Jalalabad relies on farming for subsistence. The lack of substantial irrigation systems limits subsistence farming's potential crops. Villages near the rivers and mountain streams use diversion dams that channel river or stream water into a canal system. Springs and man-made karezes channel water from underground into canal systems. Lowland areas are dotted with hundreds of individual wells using diesel water pumps to extract water for irrigation. It is estimated that 80 percent of intakes and karez systems are in need of repair or rebuilding.

## Education

Nangarhar boasts some of the highest literacy rates in Afghanistan, (56 percent of males and 18 percent of females). Jalalabad has a university, medical school, construction trades school, agriculture college, and some small training schools for English and business. There are 470 schools serving over 450,000 students spread throughout the province. Of this total, 279 have buildings, 162 have no building, and 86 schools are currently under construction. However, the schools that were built only a few years ago are overflowing, and only half the classes are held. A shortage of teachers and resources plagues the system. Although girls are allowed to attend primary school, few are able to attend high school. Nangarhar also houses a number of madrassas, which are very similar to the parochial school model in the US. The Ministry of Education is working hard to gain control of religious teaching within the country by developing "Centers of Excellence," large madrassas that provide housing and food to students.

## Healthcare

Healthcare is a key issue in Nangarhar. The quality of care is still low. Even moderately sick people often travel to Pakistan to obtain better treatment. Jalalabad has three hospitals that serve the entire Eastern Region. There are also three 40-bed hospitals in Khogiani, Shinwar, and Kama districts. There are 19 Comprehensive Health Clinics, each with 10 beds; 67 Basic Health Clinics, with out-patient care only; 12 sub-centers with very minimal care; and 750 individual health posts staffed with two volunteers each.

## PROVINCIAL RECONSTRUCTION TEAM (PRT)

The Provincial Reconstruction Team (PRT) in Nangarhar consists of a military team and three US government civilian agencies. The military side consists of a Civil Affairs (CA) team, public affairs team, engineering team, and support elements. The civilian side consists of representatives from the US Agency for International Development (USAID),

US Department of State (DoS), and US Department of Agriculture (USDA). A new partner for the PRT is the Agribusiness Development Team (ADT), made up of National Guard soldiers with several agriculture specialties.

The military wing of the PRT has focused much of its attention on building paved road systems and is now focused more on building schools. USAID has begun a new $150 million five-year program in northern, eastern, and western Afghanistan called IDEA NEW to replace the completed Alternative Development Program. USAID also has the Local Governance and Community Development program focused more on community-based projects and stability at the local governance level. The ADT focuses on agriculture and irrigation issues including watershed management and better farming methods for farmers.

## NATIONAL SOLIDARITY PROGRAM

The National Solidarity Program (NSP) is a nationwide, grass-roots development program that places development in the hands of the local populations. Community Development Councils (CDCs) prioritize, plan, and implement local development projects such as irrigation systems and small electrical systems that benefit the whole community. This program has been vastly successful due to its empowerment at the local level.

# FUTURE DEVELOPMENT IN NANGARHAR

As the chaos of the Taliban collapse recedes, future development in Nangarhar can be looked at in a much more holistic way, constantly balancing social programs with progress in infrastructure development. As provincial line directorates and district development assemblies increase their capacity, they should be involved in constructing district development plans that address all infrastructure issues. This approach could streamline development and make contracts much easier to manage by packaging projects into one contract that can be implemented at one time. When done in conjunction with line directorates and district development assemblies, it will also bring a sense of community and confidence that the government and international community are keeping their development promises. The PRT, ADT, and USAID partners have recently begun to implement this strategy.

## Table 4. UN Organizations in Nangarhar

| ACRONYM | FULL NAME | SECTORS |
|---------|-----------|---------|
| UNAMA | United Nations Mission in Afghanistan | Coordinates most UN/ NGO activities |
| UNICEF | United Nations Children's Fund | Health, education, water and sanitation program (WATSAN), and child protection |
| UNHCR | United Nations High Commissioner for Refugees | Assists refugees and returnees |
| WFP | World Food Program | Rehabilitation programs include FOODAC, food-for-work, food-for-seeds, and food-for training |
| UN-Habitat | United Nations Human Settlement Program | WATSAN, agriculture, and NSP |
| UNDP | United Nations Development Program | Support/facilitate development through: Afghan Information Management System (AIMS), Urban Development Group (UDG), National Area Based Development Program (NABDP) |
| WHO | World Health Organization | Emergency assistance, control of communicable diseases, and promotion of public health and training |
| FAO | Food Agriculture Organization | Provides agricultural inputs, such as seeds, tools, and emergency veterinary supplies/ services |
| UNOPS | United Nations Office for Project Services | Implementing construction projects of USAID and other donors |
| UNODC | United Nations Office for Drug and Crimes | Strengthens government anti-narcotic agencies |
| UNMACA | United Nations Mine Awareness and Clearance Agency | De-mining unexploded ordnance in the region |

## Table 5. International NGOs in Nangarhar

| ACRONYM | FULL NAME | MAIN ACTIVITIES |
|---|---|---|
| ACBAR | Agency Coordinating Body for Afghan Relief | Umbrella organization for NGOs in Afghanistan that does policy and advocacy work |
| AFRANE | French Afghan Friendship | Construction, education |
| AMI | Aide Medical International | Health |
| ANSO | Afghanistan Non-Governmental Organizations Security Office | Assesses the security environment for NGOs and provides up-to-date information. |
| AWC Canada | Afghan Women Council | Women's affairs, education, and vocational training for women and press |
| BRAC | Bangladesh Rural Advancement Committee | NSP assistance in health, education, agriculture, and microfinance |
| CWS | Church World Services | Health |
| DACAAR | The Danish Committee for Aid to Afghan Refugees | Water supply & sanitation |
| GAA/FSP | German Agro Action | Food security program |
| HNI | Health Net International | Health care |
| ICARDA | International Center for Agriculture Research in the Dry Areas | Rehabilitation of agriculture, livestock, and agriculture research |
| ICRC | International Committee of the Red Cross | Emergency relief for victims of armed conflicts |

| ACRONYM | FULL NAME | MAIN ACTIVITIES |
|---------|-----------|-----------------|
| IF Hope | International Foundation of Hope | Agriculture development, irrigation |
| IFRC | International Federation of Red Cross and Red Crescent Societies | Health, first aid, disaster preparedness |
| IMC | International Medical Corps | Health |
| IOC | International Orphan Care | Vocational training and education for orphans |
| IRC | International Rescue Committee | Agriculture, education small business assistance, engineering |
| ISRA | Islamic Relief Agency | Health, construction and rural development, agriculture, social welfare, and education |
| JVC | Japan International Volunteer Center | Medical mobile clinics, female education |
| MADERA | Mission d' Aide au Développement des Economies Rurales Programme Afghanistan | Agriculture, irrigation, micro-credit, and construction |
| NRC | Norwegian Refugees Council | Legal assistance, information, education |
| OMAR | Organization for Mine Clearance and Afghan Rehabilitation | Mine awareness training, health service |
| PMS (Japan) | Peshawar Medical Services | Medical services, water supply, agriculture, irrigation |

| ACRONYM | FULL NAME | MAIN ACTIVITIES |
|---------|-----------|-----------------|
| RI | Relief International | Constructs clinics, schools, marketing centers, irrigation, and microcredit |
| SAB | Solidarity Afghan Belgium | Basic education & vocational training |
| SCA | Swedish Committee for Afghanistan | Health, education, and irrigation |
| SCS | Save the Children (Sweden/Norway) | Education |
| SVA | Shanty Volunteer Organization | Education, construction |
| WAMY | World Assembly of Muslim Youth | Rehabilitation, health, and education |

*(Source: UNAMA)*

*Compared to other provinces, the media is well developed in Nangarhar, with government and private outlets for television, radio, and print. Radio is most prevelant in the province, and television is popular only in urban areas.*

PHOTO BY CAPT. DUSTIN HART

# Chapter 6
# Information and Influence

## TELECOMMUNICATIONS

There are only a few landline phones in Jalalabad. The recent expansion in cellular phone towers has connected almost every district in Nangarhar. Most youth and middle-aged people have good access to mobile phones, especially in the more populated areas. The four cellular phone systems are: Roshan Wireless, Afghan Wireless Communication Company (AWCC), Areeba, and Itsallat. Roshan and AWCC have the most customers and widest coverage areas. Since 2007, Afghan Telecom provides wireless home phone and internet service, but it is too expensive for most Afghans. There are six internet cafes in Jalalabad which charge 30 afghanis per hour with high-speed connections.

# MEDIA

The media in Nangarhar are very well developed, with government and private outlets for television, radio, and print. Most large events such as development project opening ceremonies, government meetings, and press releases are covered by multiple stations. However, journalists fear for their own safety, so they rarely discuss accusations that influential people might not agree with. The people do not always believe what they hear and have great skepticism, especially the older residents who have seen multiple governments and many propaganda campaigns. When local residents hear about promises from the government, they rarely believe the stories until they are backed up with action. They are also quick to criticize any politician they hear on the news.

## Television

Television is mostly watched in the urban areas around Jalalabad; however, some wealthier families do have televisions in the outer districts. Indian sports channels, "Bollywood" movie channels, and news channels are popular. Indian culture seems to be intriguing to most young Afghans. There are also religious channels such as "Peace TV" from India that preach moderate Islam, and American and other foreign news channels such as Al Jazeera, CNN, and Fox News.

## Radio

Radio is the most common media outlet used in the province. Over the past four years, thousands of radios have been handed out by US troops, and most people have access to one now. Major radio stations play music, host call-in shows, and spread the daily news. Although the government has its own radio station, many private stations are the favorites of the youth who were starved for music and media during the Taliban regime. RTA, Khalid, and Shaiq Radio are the most popular radio stations.

## Print

Newspapers and magazines are less prevalent in the outer areas where the literacy rates fall, but they are snatched up quickly when soldiers hand them out in villages. Several people begin reading them immediately, but others will take several papers and run back home.
It is not known how many are actually read.

### Table 6. Television Outlets

| NAME | MANAGER/ OWNER | GOVERNMENT OR PRIVATE | BROADCAST HOURS | PHONE |
|------|----------------|----------------------|-----------------|-------|
| RTA - Nangarhar | Eng. Zalmai | Government | 1200 - 2200 | 0700-655-553 |
| Shaiq Cable Network | Eng. Shafiqullah "Shaiq" | Private | 24 Hours | 0797-199-999 |
| ACTN - Cable Network | Eng. Hamayoun | Private | 24 Hours | 0773-138-284 |

## Table 7. Radio Outlets

| NAME | FREQUENCY/ BAND | MANAGER/ OWNER | GOVERNMENT OR PRIVATE | PHONE |
|------|-----------------|----------------|------------------------|-------|
| RTA - Nangarhar | 93 FM 105.2 FM 1440 AM | Eng. Zalmai | Government | 0700-655-553 |
| Shaiq Radio | 91.3 FM | Eng. Shafiqullah "Shaiq" | Private | 0797-199-999 |
| Khalid Radio | 88.00 FM | N/A | Private | N/A |
| Spinghar Radio | FM 89.04 | N/A | Private | N/A |

## Table 8. Print Outlets

| NAME | FREQUENCY | MANAGER/ OWNER | GOVERNMENT OR PRIVATE | PHONE |
|------|-----------|----------------|------------------------|-------|
| Shaiq Newspaper | 3 times per week | Eng. Shafiqullah "Shaiq" | Private | 0797-199-999 |
| Nangarhar Newspaper | 1 time per week | Awrang Smim | Government | 0700-603-576 |

## INFORMATION SHARING NETWORKS

Informal channels, including Friday sermons, are the most common method of spreading information and influencing the population outside of major towns. Prayer times at mosques, especially Friday prayers, is the time when everyone is together, gossiping, and talking about recent events. The fast spread of mobile phones has sped up the information sharing networks. Often a village will be out to greet a military convoy because someone saw it on the way and phoned ahead.

Many landowners have a small congregation area where local villagers meet to talk about the day's events, listen to radios, and gossip. Older men constantly talk about politics and corruption in the government and economic problems. Younger men talk more about education and finding a job and seem hungry for change and prosperity.

*Insurgents operate on both sides of the Durand Line, which separates Afghanistan and Pakistan. This allows insurgents to take sanctuary in the tribal agencies of Pakistan.*

PHOTO BY MICHELLE PARKER

# Chapter 7
# Big Issues

## OPIUM

The future of poppy cultivation in Nangarhar is largely dependent on future law enforcement plans, alternative development programs, and job creation. Nangarhar has bounced between being one of the biggest poppy growing provinces to being relatively poppy free in the past few years. Currently, Nangarhar is growing negligible amounts of poppy, but that could change any season. For example, in 2007, Nangarhar went from growing 4,000 hectares of poppy to 18,000 hectares in one season. A continued focus on building irrigation, road, and power infrastructure and on providing alternative crops and agribusiness will continue to stem the growth of poppy.

## POROUS BORDER

The porous border with Pakistan is a major obstacle for stability in Nangarhar. The open border creates the opportunity for insurgents to enter Nangarhar, attack government officials and international workers, and retreat back into the safe haven of the FATA in Pakistan. Training and equipping the Border Police helps to stop some incursions, but there are still many challenges to shutting down the border to insurgents.

Smuggling goods in and out of Afghanistan is often done through border crossing points as well, typically in the southeastern area of Nangarhar. In order to avoid high tariffs on imports to Pakistan, traders who bring their goods through the port in Karachi mark the boxes for export to Afghanistan. Goods are then sent through the border at Torkham Gate in Nangarhar without examination because they are marked for Afghanistan. After the cargo passes through the border, it is offloaded and smuggled back into Pakistan. Smuggling opium and heroin out of Nangarhar is also done using the same smuggling routes.

## REFUGEE/RETURNEE ISSUES

Millions of refugees fled Afghanistan over the past three decades because of war and strife. Camp closures by the Pakistani government and the desire to return home caused many people to return through Torkham Gate and set up residence in Nangarhar. Many of the returnees were not from Nangarhar, but from other provinces in the Eastern Region. This flood of returnees exacerbated many of the problems Nangarhar already faced.

The government has worked hard to assist the returnees from other provinces back to their home of origin, but many have stayed in Nangarhar. Due to this influx of returnees, large land areas were given to these people to settle. One of these areas was Sheik Mesri in Surkh Rod district, which has ballooned in population from a few hundred people to thousands of people over the past three years. This has created unemployment, and the area lacks the infrastructure to support this population increase.

## DEVELOPMENT SURGE

After seven years of international military and civilian presence in Nangarhar, the local population, especially the rural population, is frustrated with the slow pace of development. Afghans had very high expectations that their needs would be met and their lives would change for the better in a very short time.

After the rout of the Taliban in 2002 and in the absence of an organized insurgency, assistance efforts in rural areas focused on traditional development, especially the basic infrastructure devastated by the war (i.e., roads and power) and restoring structures to provide basic social services (i.e., government buildings, schools, and clinics). The historic model of development used in Nangarhar included taking requests from communities, government leaders, and maliks and building based on these requests. As those projects have progressed and the Taliban and other anti-government forces have returned, the coalition's efforts have become focused on counterinsurgency projects with varying degrees of success.

Currently, there is an unprecedented influx of resources. CERP resources in Nangarhar have gone from $4 million in 2005 to nearly $100 million this year, and USAID is now starting a new $150 million plan throughout much of the country. This increase is allowing the military to surge development into sectors such as paved roads, which were too expensive only three years ago. The PRT has addressed most of the road systems with a multi-million dollar plan to pave all major road in the province. The PRT is now taking that same holistic approach to school building. Instead of identifying a small number of schools and building them based on requests, the PRT is working with the director of education to prioritize and build over 100 schools in the most needed areas. Similarly, the ADT is working with the directors of irrigation and agriculture to identify and build all of the karez and spring irrigation systems that have been neglected for decades.

Providing electrical power can be a lever to gain support from local officials. Unfortunately, getting power to rural areas is extremely difficult. One possible solution is micro-hydro power. The Counternarcotics Advisory Team (CNAT) is taking the lead in the rural power sector by identifying every possible location that micro-hydro power systems can be built and building at least 50 of them this year.

*While appreciative of the work ethic and sacrifices shown by members of the US armed forces, Afghans often complain that coalition forces and international personnel do not understand the local people and what is happening among them.*

PHOTO BY SPC HAROLD FIELDS

# Appendices

## TIMELINE OF MAJOR EVENTS

**Spring 2005:**

- Poppy cultivation levels drop from 20,000 hectares to 1,500 hectares in one year after a large tribal shura convinces the population to give up poppy in return for development.

- USAID begins a five-year, $150 million Alternative Development Program to bring major development to the Eastern Region.

- Riots take place in Jalalabad in protest of the false reports that soldiers flushed a Koran down a toilet in Guantanamo Bay prison. The rioters burn many government buildings and UN compounds before order is restored.

**Fall 2005:** Gul Agha Sherzai becomes governor of Nangarhar. PC and parliamentary elections take place for the first time in decades. The Nangarhar population had a high turnout amid optimism for the future.

**Spring 2006:** A Roads Working Group is set up between all government and non-government organizations in Nangarhar. This led to an ongoing, comprehensive plan that has reconstructed most major road systems in Nangarhar.

**Spring 2007:** Poppy cultivation rises again to over 18,000 hectares. The population claims that development promises were not kept by the government and international community.

**Fall 2007:** A Marine convoy is attacked by bombs and small arms fire on the main Jalalabad-Torkham highway. Reports claimed that the Marines responded by killing several civilians, creating widespread animosity toward the US military in Nangarhar.

**Fall 2008:** Governor Sherzai promises increased development and cracks down on farmers cultivating poppy. Nangarhar poppy cultivation falls to only 35 hectares and Nangarhar is declared "poppy free" for the first time since the fall of the Taliban.

**Spring 2009:** PC member Qasi Khan Mohammad and Goshta district sub-governor Haji Naeem are assassinated on the same day. Although the motives are not known, political posturing is assumed to be the reason.

## COMMON COMPLIMENTS REGARDING THE US MILITARY IN THE EASTERN REGION

- Afghans compliment the US forces' work ethic and say it drives them to work harder for themselves.

- Afghans are happy with projects such as roads that change their lives for the better after decades of war.

- Afghans respect the US forces for leaving their families to come and help them.

## COMMON COMPLAINTS REGARDING THE US MILITARY IN THE EASTERN REGION

- Afghans claim that US forces have inflicted excessive civilian casualties while taking out few insurgent leaders.

- Afghans complain that the US forces raid their houses at night without cause or government support.

- Afghans believe Americans use informers for their intelligence gathering who are not being honest. Most of these people have their own agendas and manipulate the truth.

- Afghans lament that coalition forces and other foreign personnel do not know or understand the local people and what is going on among them.

- Afghans complain when US forces drive them off the roads and drive too carelessly.


## DAY IN THE LIFE OF A RURAL NANGARHARI

The schedule of daily life in rural Nangarhar depends on the season. Country people rise before dawn to offer the first of their five daily prayers. Women build a fire over which they cook flat loaves of bread in the tandoor, a stone oven. Breakfast typically consists of bread mashed in milk, or bread with cheese or curds, washed down with milk tea. During the spring and summer growing season, the women set out to the fields to spend their day weeding, fertilizing, and irrigating. Before noon, they pause to eat a small snack of bread and say their midday prayers before returning to their arduous agricultural work. At dusk they return home to cook dinner, which usually consists of more bread, different vegetables based on the season, and yogurt milk. Meat is not routinely eaten, but is reserved for special occasions. In the spring, wild greens supplement the meal; later in the season, beans, peas, and squash are also eaten.

Men are in charge of the livestock, which many families own for milk. The cows feed off the corn and wheat stalks after harvest and graze in mountain pastures. During the summer months, the men spend their days in the pastures, herding the goats on their daily grazing rounds and producing the various types of cheese and curds derived from the animals' milk. Several men will pool their livestock and manpower resources, taking turns with the chores.

During the fall, women spend their days gathering firewood for the next season's heating and cooking. In winter months, after harvesting and settling in, daily life slows. Women tend to household chores; men hang out around the mosque or with friends, playing games or just talking about everyday events.

## READING LIST

### Books

- Ahmed Rashid, *Taliban: Militant Islam, Oil, and Fundamentalism in Central Asia*, 2001.

- Ahmed Rashid, *Descent into Chaos: The US and the Disaster in Pakistan, Afghanistan, and Central Asia*, New York: Penguin Group, 2008.

- Barnett Rubin, *The Fragmentation of Afghanistan*, 2001.

- Barnett Rubin, *Afghanistan's Uncertain Transition from Turmoil to Normalcy*, 2007.

- Ben Macintyre, *The Man Who Would Be King, The First American in Afghanistan*, New York: Farrar, Straus, and Giroux, 2005.

- Edward Girardet and Jonathan Walter, *Afghanistan: Essential Field Guides to Humanitarian and Conflict Zones*, CROSSLINES Publication Ltd., 1998 and 2004. *www.crosslinesguides.com*

- Greg Mortenson, *Three Cups of Tea: One Man's Mission to Promote Peace...One School at a Time,* 2007. (excellent understanding of how to succeed with the people and culture)

- Larry Goodson, *Afghanistan's Endless War: State Failure, Regional Politics, and the Rise of the Taliban*, 2001.

- Louis Dupree, *Afghanistan*, Princeton: Princeton University Press, 1979.

- Michael Griffin, *Reaping the Whirlwind; The Taliban Movement in Afghanistan*, London: Pluto Press, 2001.

- Sarah Chayes, *The Punishment of Virtue: Inside Afghanistan After the Taliban*, New York: Penguin Group, 2007.

- Steve Coll, *Ghost Wars: The Secret History of the CIA, Afghanistan, and Bin Laden, From the Soviet Invasion to September 10, 2001*, New York Penguin Press, 2004.

- *ISAF PRT Handbook*, 3rd Ed. February 2007. NATO.

## Articles

- President Karzai, "The Afghanistan National Development Strategy," 2006. *www.reliefweb.int/rw/RWFiles2006.nsf/ FilesByRWDocUNIDFileName/KHII-6LK3R2-unama-afg-30jan2. pdf/$File/unama-afg-30jan2.pdf*

- Afghanistan Research and Evaluation Unit, "Elections in 2009 and 2010: Technical and Contextual Challenges to Building Democracy in Afghanistan," November 2008. *www.areu.org. af/index.php?option=com_docman&Itemid=26&task=doc_ download&gid=612*

- Raphy Favre, "Potential Analysis of the Eastern Region and Nangarhar Province and Implication in Programming," *www.aizon.org/Nangarhar%20Potential%20Analysis.pdf*

- G.H. Orris and J.D. Bliss, "Mines and Mineral Occurrences of Afghanistan - Open Report 02-110," US Geological Survey, US Department of the Interior, 2002.

## Websites

- Afghanistan Research and Evaluation Unit (publishes the Afghanistan A to Z guide), *www.areu.org.af/index. php?option=com_frontpage&Itemid=25*

- Afghanistan Information Management Services, *www.aims.org.af*

- Afghanistan Online (Links to Official IRA and embassy websites), *www.afghan-web.com/politics*

- Naval Postgraduate School Program for Culture and Conflict Studies, *www.nps.edu/Programs/CCS/index.html*

- USAID, *www.usaid.gov/locations/asia/countries/afghanistan*

www.ingramcontent.com/pod-product-compliance
Lightning Source LLC
Chambersburg PA
CBHW040512290326
R18043100001B/R180431PG41927CBX00001B/1